COMPANION WORKBOOK - THE BLISS PROTOCOL

COMPANION WORKBOOK - THE BLISS PROTOCOL

KOFIE AND LACHELE BRYANT

THE BLISS PROTOCOL WORKBOOK

Introduction:

Welcome to "The Bliss Protocol" workbook. This companion guide is designed to help you and your spouse apply the principles from Kofie and Lachele Bryant's book to your own marriage. Each chapter contains reflective questions, exercises, and activities to deepen your understanding and strengthen your relationship.

How to use this workbook:

1. Read the corresponding chapter in "The Bliss Protocol"
2. Complete the exercises individually, then discuss them together
3. Be honest, open, and respectful in your responses
4. Revisit exercises periodically to track your growth
5. You may need additional paper so have a journal to track your progress and complete the exercises.

Remember, this is a journey. Take your time, be patient with each other, and celebrate your progress along the way.

1

Family Lyfe

Crafting Harmony Within Blended Families

PRINCIPLE: "Harmony in diversity fosters unity in love"
BLISS PROTOCOL #10: Embracing Difference

Reflection Questions:
1. What challenges have you faced in blending your families?

----

2. How have your family dynamics changed since getting married?

_____
_____
_____
_____
_____

3. What traditions from each of your backgrounds do you want to maintain?
_____
_____
_____
_____
_____

Exercise: Creating a Family Values Statement

1. Individually, list 5-10 values that are important to you in family life.
_____
_____
_____
_____
_____

2. Share your lists and circle the values that overlap.
_____
_____
_____
_____
_____

3. Discuss and agree on 5-7 core values for your blended family.
_____
_____
_____
_____
_____

4. Write a statement that incorporates these values and how you'll live them out.

Activity: Mapping Your Blended Family Tree

Materials needed: Large paper, markers

1. Draw your family tree, including all members of your blended family.
2. Use different colors to represent different family units.
3. Add symbols to represent strong relationships, areas of tension, etc.
4. Discuss your tree together, identifying areas for growth and celebration.

2

BLISS

Cultivating Serenity in the Spirit-Filled Home

PRINCIPLE: "True understanding stems from the heart's ability to listen; compassionate communication forges unbreakable bonds of spiritual intimacy.

BLISS PROTOCOL #2: The Art of Intentional Listening

Meditation Exercise for Couples:
1. Sit comfortably facing each other.
2. Hold hands and close your eyes.
3. Focus on your breath for 1 minute.
4. Silently send loving thoughts to your partner for 2 minutes.
5. Open your eyes and share your experience.

Worksheet: Identifying Sources of Stress and Serenity in Your Home
List sources of:

Stress:

Serenity:

Discuss: How can you minimize stress and maximize serenity?

Activity: Creating a Spiritual Practice Together

1. List individual spiritual practices you each enjoy.

---

2. Circle practices you'd like to try together.

_____
_____

3. Create a weekly schedule incorporating at least one shared spiritual practice.
_____
_____
_____
_____
_____

3

Can We All Get Along

Cultivating Compassionate Communication

PRINCIPLE: A home bathed in spirituality and love becomes a sanctuary of peace; every room echoes with harmony, and every corner is filled with bliss.

BLISS PROTOCOL #12: Spiritual Connection

Communication Style Assessment:

Rate yourself from 1 (never) to 5 (always):

__ I express my feelings openly.

__ I listen without interrupting.

__ I ask for clarification when unsure.

__ I avoid blame and criticism.

__ I express appreciation regularly.

Discuss your results and areas for improvement.

Role-playing Exercises for Active Listening:

1. Partner A shares a minor frustration for 2 minutes.

2. Partner B listens without interrupting, then summarizes what they heard.

3. Switch roles and repeat.

Journaling Prompts for Expressing Feelings:

1. When I feel misunderstood, I...

_____
_____
_____
_____
_____

2. I feel most loved when my partner...

_____
_____
_____
_____
_____

3. A recent time I felt deeply connected to my partner was...

_____
_____
_____
_____
_____

Share your responses with each other.

4

Unity in Intimacy

Embracing the Spirit

PRINCIPLE: "Conflict, when navigated with love and respect, becomes a canvas for growth and deeper connection."

BLISS PROTOCOL #13: Healthy Conflict, Deeper Understanding

Intimacy Inventory Questionnaire:

Rate your satisfaction from 1 (very dissatisfied) to 5 (very satisfied):
__ Physical intimacy
__ Emotional intimacy
__ Spiritual intimacy
__ Intellectual intimacy

__ Recreational intimacy

Discuss areas where you align and differ.

Exercise: Exploring Love Languages Together

1. Take the Five Love Languages quiz online.

2. Share your results with each other.

3. List 3 ways you can show love in your partner's primary language.

Activity: Creating an Intimacy Vision Board

Materials needed: Magazines, scissors, glue, poster board

1. Cut out images and words that represent your ideal intimate relationship.

2. Arrange and glue these onto the poster board.

3. Present your vision board to each other, explaining your choices.

4. Display the board where you'll see it regularly.

5

I See You

The Art of Constructive Conflict

PRINCIPLE "Intimacy is the soul's language of love; true unity is found when two hearts communicate beyond the physical."

BLISS PROTOCOL #5: Love Languages 2.0

Conflict Resolution Style Assessment:
For each scenario, choose your most likely response:
A. Avoid the issue
B. Compromise
C. Collaborate to find a win-win
D. Compete to win
E. Accommodate the other person
1. Disagreement over finances: __

2. Difference in parenting styles: __
3. Conflict over household chores: __

Discuss your patterns and how they impact your relationship.

Worksheet: Identifying Common Triggers and Solutions

List your top 3 conflict triggers:

_____
_____
_____

For each trigger, brainstorm 2-3 potential solutions.

_____
_____
_____
_____
_____

Practice Scenarios for Applying Constructive Conflict Techniques:

1. Role-play a common conflict in your relationship.
2. Use "I" statements to express feelings.
3. Practice active listening and summarizing.
4. Work together to find a mutually satisfactory solution.

6

Embracing Unified Purpose

We Are In This Together

PRINCIPLE: In unity, there is abundance; aligning spiritual and financial growth paves the way for a thriving union.

BLISS PROTOCOL #16: Creating Shared Rituals

Goal-setting Worksheet for Couples:

Short-term goals (1 year):

Long-term goals (5+ years):

_____
_____
_____
_____
_____

Exercise: Aligning Individual and Shared Dreams

1. Individually, write down your top 3 personal dreams.

WIFE:
_____
_____
_____
_____
_____

HUSBAND:
_____
_____
_____
_____
_____

2. Share these with your partner.
3. Identify how your individual dreams can support or complement each other.
4. Create 3 shared dreams that incorporate elements from both of your visions.
_____
_____
_____
_____
_____

Activity: Creating a Shared Mission Statement

1. Individually, complete the sentence: "Our purpose as a couple is to..."

_____
_____
_____
_____
_____

2. Share your statements and circle keywords or phrases that resonate.

_____
_____
_____
_____
_____

3. Craft a joint mission statement using these key elements.

_____
_____
_____
_____
_____

4. Write your mission statement on a card and place it somewhere visible.

_____
_____
_____
_____
_____

7

Flourishing in Shared Abundance

What's Mine is Yours and What's Yours is Mine

PRINCIPLE: "Two souls, one journey; embracing a unified purpose is the essence of true partnership."

BLISS PROTOCOL #1: Rediscovering Your Why

Financial Values Assessment:

Rank the following from 1 (least important) to 10 (most important):
__ Security
__ Freedom
__ Generosity
__ Status
__ Growth
__ Responsibility

__ Enjoyment

__ Legacy

__ Simplicity

__ Adventure

Discuss how your values align or differ.

Budgeting Exercise for Couples:

1. List all sources of income.

2. List all expenses, categorizing them as needs or wants.

3. Allocate percentages to saving, giving, and spending.

4. Create a plan for tracking expenses together.

Activity: Creating a Shared Abundance Mindset

1. List 5 ways you feel abundant in your life right now.

2. Share a time when you experienced unexpected abundance.

3. Create a gratitude practice to acknowledge daily abundance.

8

Nurturing

Growing the Physical and Spiritual Well Being

PRINCIPLE "Well-being is a harmonious blend of physical health and spiritual depth; nurturing both leads to a flourishing life together."

BLISS PROTOCOL #15: Self-Love and Self-Care

Wellness Check-in Questionnaire:

Rate your satisfaction from 1 (very dissatisfied) to 5 (very satisfied):

__ Physical health

__ Mental health

__ Emotional well-being

__ Spiritual growth

__ Work-life balance

Discuss areas for improvement and how you can support each other.

Exercise: Creating a Couple's Health and Wellness Plan

1. Set 3 health goals you'd like to achieve together.

_____
_____
_____
_____
_____

2. List activities you enjoy doing together that promote wellness.
_____
_____
_____
_____
_____

3. Create a weekly schedule incorporating these activities.
_____
_____
_____
_____
_____

Activity: Designing Spiritual Growth Practices Together
1. List spiritual practices that are meaningful to you individually.
_____
_____
_____
_____
_____

2. Identify practices you'd like to try or deepen together.
_____
_____
_____
_____
_____

3. Commit to a shared spiritual practice for the next 30 days.
_____
_____
_____
_____
_____

9

Cultivating Mindful Wealth Management

Developing a Healthy Mindset

PRINCIPLE: Financial prosperity flourishes in the garden of mindfulness; intertwining acumen with awareness cultivates a stable future.

BLISS PROTOCOL #11: Shared Vision Ques

Financial Goal-setting Worksheet:
Short-term financial goals (1 year):

Long-term financial goals (5+ years):

_____
_____
_____
_____

Exercise: Aligning Spiritual Values with Financial Decisions

1. List your top 3 spiritual values.
_____
_____
_____
_____
_____

2. For each value, identify how it can guide your financial choices.
_____
_____
_____
_____
_____

3. Create a set of financial principles based on these values.
_____
_____
_____
_____
_____

Activity: Creating a Legacy Planning Timeline

1. Envision your desired legacy 20+ years from now.
2. Work backward, setting milestones for 15, 10, and 5 years from now.
3. Identify actions you can take this year to move towards your legacy goals.

10

Cultivating Collective Joy

Joy is Different from Happy

PRINCIPLE: "Collective joy is the tapestry of shared experiences; woven with threads of community and friendship, it enriches the soul and strengthens bonds."

BLISS PROTOCOL #7: Shared Adventures

Social Network Mapping Exercise:
1. Draw a circle representing you as a couple in the center of a page.
2. Add circles for different social groups (family, friends, church, etc.).
3. Draw lines connecting you to these groups, thicker lines for stronger connections.
4. Identify areas where you'd like to strengthen or expand your social network.
Worksheet: Planning Shared Experiences and Adventures
1. List activities you both enjoy.

----

2. Identify new experiences you'd like to try together.

----

3. Plan one new shared adventure for each month of the coming year.

Activity:
Creating a "Joy Jar" for Collecting Happy Moments
Materials needed: A large jar, small pieces of paper, pens
1. Decorate your jar together.
2. Each day, write down one thing that brought you joy as a couple.
3. At the end of each month, read through your joy notes together.

11

Expanding the Circle of Trust

Trust in God First

PRINCIPLE: "Trust weaves the fabric of communal bonds; expanding our circle invites a tapestry of support and shared joy."

BLISS PROTOCOL #3: Vulnerability and Authenticity

Trust-building Exercises for Couples:
1. Eye contact exercise: Maintain eye contact for 2 minutes without speaking.
2. Trust fall: Take turns catching each other (ensure safety).
3. Vulnerability share: Each partner shares something they find difficult to talk about.
Worksheet: Identifying and Nurturing Key Relationships
1. List the 5 most important relationships in your lives (outside of each other).

_____
_____
_____
_____
_____

2. For each relationship, identify how you can nurture it as a couple.
_____
_____
_____
_____
_____

3. Create an action plan to strengthen one key relationship this month.
_____
_____
_____
_____
_____

Activity: Planning a Community Engagement Project Together
1. Identify a need in your community.
_____
_____
_____
_____

2. Brainstorm ways you could address this need as a couple.
_____
_____
_____
_____
_____

3. Create an action plan to implement your community project.

12

Building Legacy and Leadership

In Order to Lead You Must Be Able to Follow

PRINCIPLE: Building Legacy and Leadership

BLISS PROTOCOL #23: Shared Purpose, Shared Service

Leadership Style Assessment for Couples:

Rate yourself from 1 (never) to 5 (always):
__ I lead by example.
__ I empower others.
__ I communicate vision clearly.
__ I adapt to changing situations.
__ I take responsibility for outcomes.

Discuss how your leadership styles complement each other.

Exercise: Crafting Your Shared Leadership Vision

1. Individually, write your definition of effective leadership.

HUSBAND: _____
_____

WIFE: _____
_____

2. Share and discuss your definitions.
_____
_____
_____
_____
_____

3. Create a joint leadership philosophy that incorporates both perspectives.
_____
_____
_____
_____
_____

Activity: Creating a Legacy Project Plan

1. Identify a cause or issue you're both passionate about.
_____
_____
_____
_____

2. Envision a project that could make a lasting impact in this area.
3. Outline the steps needed to bring this project to life.
4. Set a timeline for implementing your legacy project.

Conclusion:

Reflection on the Journey:
1. What was the most impactful exercise for you?
2. How has this workbook strengthened your relationship?
3. What areas do you want to continue working on together?

13

Commitment Ceremony Script

PERSONALIZE THIS SCRIPT AND USE IT TO RECOMMIT TO EACH OTHER AND YOUR SHARED VISION

"I, [Name], recommit myself to you, [Partner's Name], and to our shared journey of love, growth, and purpose. I promise to continue nurturing our relationship, supporting your dreams as my own, and working alongside you to build our legacy of love and impact. With gratitude for our past, joy in our present, and hope for our future, I choose you again and always."

Next Steps for Continued Growth and Bliss in Marriage:

1. Schedule regular check-ins to revisit these exercises.
2. Choose one area each month to focus on improving together.
3. Celebrate your progress and love for each other often.

Remember, "The Bliss Protocol" is not just a destination, but a lifelong journey of love, growth, and shared purpose. May your path be filled with joy, understanding, and endless discovery.

www.ingramcontent.com/pod-product-compliance
Lightning Source LLC
Chambersburg PA
CBHW081504070526
44586CB00019B/2471